The Sun Is Up

by Lada Josefa Kratky

NATIONAL
GEOGRAPHIC

School Publishing

Come and sit here.
Look at the sun come up.

The sun is up a little bit.
What time is it now?
It is five.

How did the sun get that
size? What time is it now?
It is six.

Now it is nine. Come on,
we can hike.

We got to the top! Look at the sun now! How did it get there?

How did the sun get there?
And how did it get there?

I can not find the sun now.
How did the sun hide? How?